Dad, You're Not Funny
and Other Poems

STEVE TURNER

Illustrations by David Mostyn

Dad, You're Not Funny and Other Poems

LION
Children's Books

THE OTHER POEMS ARE FUNNY.

**For Paul Crankshaw,
my companion on so many
childhood escapades**

Text copyright © 1999 Steve Turner
Illustrations copyright © 1999 David Mostyn
This edition copyright © 2000 Lion Publishing

The moral rights of the author and illustrator
have been asserted

Published by
Lion Publishing plc
Sandy Lane West, Oxford, England
www.lion-publishing.co.uk
ISBN 0 7459 4025 0

First edition 1999
First paperback edition 2000
10 9 8 7 6 5 4 3

A catalogue record for this book is available
from the British Library

Typeset in 12/auto Latin 725 MdBT
Printed and bound in Great Britain by
Cox & Wyman, Reading

Contents

Introduction

Ladies and Gentlemen

News and Weather

Body and Spirit

Animals and Insects

Thoughts and Dreams

Introduction

Welcome to my new book of poetry. I hope that you'll enjoy it. The title comes from something my son, Nathan, says when I make jokes – especially when I try to make him laugh in front of his friends, and even more especially if I try to make his friends laugh in front of him.

The first question I get asked when I read my work in schools is – Where do you get your ideas from? So let me explain how I came to write Dad, You're Not Funny.

A lot of the poems are about when I was young. I wrote them because even though much has changed since then (like the fashions we wear), I'm sure that the things we dream about and worry about are the same.

Some of the other poems were stimulated by a book for teachers that suggested subjects for poetry. I would choose something from a long list and go away and write a poem that fitted. It can be surprising what ideas we've got tucked away in the backs of our minds that we only become aware of when we're given a challenge. How else would I have thought of writing about wheels or hands, for example?

I hope that reading these poems will bring you as much pleasure as I have had writing them. Why not share them with your friends and family?

Family and Friends

The Best Dad

My dad's much weaker than your dad
My dad's got less hair on his head
My dad snores louder than your dad
My dad spends more time in bed.

My dad's much weirder than your dad
My dad's got more flakes up his nose
My dad's less trendy than your dad
My dad wears more awful clothes.

My dad's more sober than your dad
My dad's got more wax in his ears
My dad talks dafter than your dad
My dad looks older by years.

My dad's got less teeth than your dad
My dad's got more sweat in his pits
My dad's much plumper than your dad
That's why I love him to bits.

Dad, You're Not Funny

A few of my mates
Come around to our place
And you're at the door
With a grin on your face.
You know that I know
You're a really good bloke,
But I'll curl up and die
If you tell us a joke.

We don't want to hear
About your days at school,
We don't want to watch
You try to be cool.
We don't want to know
How the world used to be.
We don't want to see
Those videos of me.

We don't want to laugh
At your riddles and rhymes,
At musty old tales
We've heard fifty times.
We don't want a quiz
Where we have to compete,
We don't want to guess
Why the hen crossed the street.

Please don't perform
That ridiculous dance
Like you did on the night
We went out in France.
Don't do impressions
Of pop stars on drugs.
Whatever you do
Don't swamp me with hugs.

So Dad, don't come in,
Your jokes are so dated
I often pretend
That we're not related.
I'd pay you to hide
If I had my own money
The simple truth is –
Dad, you're not funny.

Cranky, Scotty, Mooey and Me

We form a secret club,
Cranky, Scotty, Mooey and me,
with passwords
    secret signs
    membership
    a magazine
and a language
only we can understand.

We need a meeting place,
Cranky, Scotty, Mooey and me.
Cranky says a den
Scotty says a barn
I say a shed
and Mooey says
    a secret island
    surrounded by trees.

CRANKY

SCOTTY

A secret island surrounded by trees!
A secret island surrounded by trees? say
Cranky, Scotty and me.
Yes, says Mooey
who draws a map of
  a field
  a wood
  a bridge
  and an island marked X.

Mooey's idea is voted on by
Cranky, Scotty, Mooey and me.
It wins 4-0.
It sounds just like
  William
  Treasure Island
  The Famous Five
  The Secret Seven.

MOOEY

ME

The next weekend we meet up,
Cranky, Scotty, Mooey and me.
We hike over fields
    climb fences
    open gates
    skirt woods
    walk up hills
and then, below us, we see
the glint of water through leaves.
It's the secret lake
around the secret island.

We cut ourselves sticks to beat back the undergrowth,
Cranky, Scotty, Mooey and me.
Then it's right there in front of us
    with overhanging trees
    thick green rushes
    and a rickety wooden bridge.

At this point you expect something bad to happen to
Cranky, Scotty, Mooey and me.
Like, we all wake up and find that it's a dream
　　　the lake turns out to be a puddle
　　　the island is a mole hill
　　　or the whole thing is a film set.

But it wasn't that way for
Cranky, Scotty, Mooey and me.
It was a real island
　　　in a real lake
　　　hidden in a real wood
and no one knew about it
　　　but us.

We sat in the bushes,
Cranky, Scotty, Mooey and me,
　　　listening to ducks
　　　watching gnats hit water
　　　thinking about treasure
wondering if life was always
this perfect.

Sue Was Two

Sue was two
and didn't talk.
I was five and did.
Our Sue sat
in her high chair
with mashed-up food and bib.

Mum stood up
and left the room.
'Behave yourselves,' she said.
When she'd gone
I took the lunch
and tipped it on Sue's head.

Food ran down
her baby cheeks
and stuck inside her hair.
Sue cried out
and Mum rushed in
and pulled her from her chair.

I just sat
as good as gold
while Sue took all the blame.
It felt good
when I was five
but now I feel ashamed.

Ten Things Mums Never Say

1. Keep your mouth open when you eat,
    then you'll be able to talk at the same time.

2. Jump down the stairs.
    It's quicker than walking.

3. Don't eat all your vegetables.
    You won't have enough room for your sweets.

4. It's too early for bed.
    Stay up and watch more television.

5. Be rude to your teachers.
    It would be dishonest to be polite.

6. By all means walk on the furniture.
    It's already badly scratched.

7. Don't brush your teeth.
    They'll only get dirty again.

8. It's not your fault that your pocket money
    only lasts for a day.

9. Wipe your feet on the sofas.
    That's what they're there for.

10. I was far worse behaved than you
    when I was young.

When Grandad Comes to Stay

We must be well-behaved
When Grandad comes to stay
No sliding down the staircase
Until he goes away
No running in the hall
Or playing games like chase
We have to clean our ears
And keep a well-scrubbed face.

We have to be so quiet
When Grandad's in his chair
We have to sneak around
As if we're hardly there
We can't play our CDs
Or punch each other's heads
We have to clean our rooms
And make up our own beds.

We need to be polite
When Grandad comes to us
No burping during mealtimes
Or letting slip a cuss
We must say please and thank you
And could you pass the cup
Then Grandad will believe that
We've all been well brought up.

Kisses

Father's kiss
is leathery.
Mother's kiss
is silk.
Our cat
gives me kisses
as if she's
lapping milk.

Sister's kiss
is slobbery.
Brother's kiss
is weak.
A kiss from
our canary
is a tickle
from a beak.

Grandad's kiss
is whiskery.
Nanna's kiss
is wet.
A kiss from
Father Christmas
is the prickliest
you'll get.

NOBODY EVER KISSES ME.

Shopping with Mum

I'm so bored with supermarkets
They almost send me mad,
If I don't get some chocolate
I could do something quite bad,
I could knock into the noodles
And lash into the leeks,
So, hurry up, Mum,
I WANT MY SWEETS!

I could batter the bananas
And pulverise a plum,
I could kick a bunch of carrots
And wreck a rack of rum,
I could whack a box of Weetabix
And shake a Shredded Wheat,
So, hurry up, Mum,
I WANT MY SWEETS!

I could chuck a chunk of cheese
And topple all the tins,
I could wrestle with a rissole
And bash a load of bins,
I could crack a Coca Cola
And bang a sugar beet,
So, hurry up, Mum,
I WANT MY SWEETS!

I could biff a load of biscuits
And grab a jar of jam,
I could monkey with the marmalade
And lump a leg of lamb,
I could pinch a piece of pasta
And punch a plate of meat,
So, hurry up, Mum,
I WANT MY SWEETS!

Best Friends

Best friends tell you secrets
Best friends always play
Best friends send you postcards
When they go away.

Best friends guess your thinking
Best friends read your eyes
Best friends notice right away
If you're telling lies.

Best friends say they're sorry
Best friends say they care
Best friends may be absent
But they're always there.

Fun and Games

The Flying Wheel

Stand on a cliff top
Pull on the string
The circle of red
Turns into a wing.

Flies like a seagull
Up in the blue
Turns into a dot
Glides out of view.

Stand on a cliff top
Look in the sky
All that is red
Spins from the eye.

Call of the seagull
Crash of the wave
The circle of red
Falls to its grave.

Pocket Money

It's dark living in a pocket or purse,
but it's warm.
You get to meet other coins
of all shapes and sizes.
Sometimes an American dollar
or a Portuguese escudo drops in.
When people sit down
you can rest and chat
but if they run and jump
you bounce up and down
until you're almost sick.
Some people have a habit
of 'playing with their change'
– grabbing us, squeezing us
and throwing us around in
the dark.
It can be quite scary.
It can make you long for
the security of a slot machine
where you slide down a tunnel
and live in a comfortable steel box
for several days.
Being a coin is interesting.
It involves a lot of travel,
a lot of sweat
and everyone is always
glad to see you.
Humans, it is said, will do
anything for money.

The best moment in my life
was appearing at the Cup Final.
It was painful –
I got flicked on my tail
and ended face down on the pitch –
but I was cheered by 80,000 people
and was seen briefly on TV.
When I retire I'd like to be
part of a special collection,
resting on a satin cushion
inside a silver box.

Mud

In the days before computers
we had mud.
You couldn't send messages
on mud
but you could play games on it.
On Saturday mornings
we went looking for mud
– great piles of fresh mud
straight from the builder's truck;
mud we made ourselves
from soil and water;
mud scooped from the beds of
ponds and streams.
We ran through mud
and jumped in mud.
We clambered up mud
and slid down mud.
We rolled in mud and
sat on mud.
Grown-ups didn't like mud.
They wouldn't allow it in the house.
They wore protective clothing,
they scrubbed it off trousers
and washed it off cars.
But I liked mud.
You couldn't save data on mud
but there were many different levels
and it was always dirt cheap.

Digging a Hole

Digging and digging
I feel like a failure.
I've dug for three days
And I can't find Australia.

Travel Game

Sitting on buses
or in the back seats of cars
I pass the time
by imagining a huge scythe
jutting out like a wing.
As we speed along,
this curved blade slices through
all that it meets.
Telegraph poles tumble,
trees become stumps,
hedgerows are trimmed
to the length of new grass.
Nothing is too tough
for my imaginary scythe.
It hacks through hills,
slides through steel
and breaks through bricks.
I see tower blocks become bungalows,
houses become huts
and mountains become molehills,
as hours are chopped down to minutes
and seconds are whittled away.

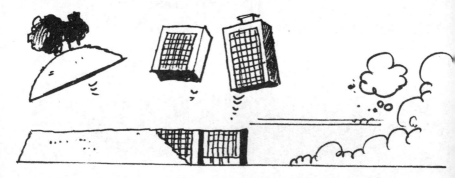

The Monarch

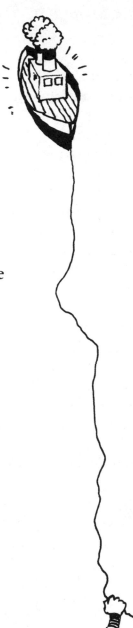

Dad built me a ship
And painted it green
It sailed in on wheels
That couldn't be seen.

Treacle-tin funnels
Puffed white cotton wool
Copper-coin capstans
Gave thick string a pull.

Torch bulbs in cabins
Through portholes would shine
This was the *Monarch*
And this ship was mine.

I tugged at its bow
And it ploughed down the hall
On oceans of tile
Past coastlines of wall.

Up tempest staircase
Then out of the depths
I'd anchor it near
The bed where I slept.

I'd flick on the switch
To fill it with light
Then lie in the dark
And watch it at night.

Knocking on Doors

Before TV,
In days of old,
When I was a bouncing boy,
We made our own
Amusements up
And found new ways to annoy.

Knocking on doors
And running away
Try getting us if you dare.
You won't catch us
'less you take a bus
And you can't afford the fare.

Bundles of string
And sticks and stuff
For rattles and rings and knocks.
Nails to dangle
On window panes
And bangers to post through a box.

Knocking on doors
And running away etc.

Cranky and me,
On our way home,
Give an old door a kick
A man leaps out
I hear his boots
Hitting the road with a click.

Knocking on doors
And running away etc.

The two of us
Begin to run
But Cranky begins too late.
I see the man,
He reaches us
And Cranky awaits his fate.

Knocking on doors
And running away etc.

Cranky's grabbed
Around the neck
And dragged along the street,
Then marched in to
A living room
By the man with clicking feet.

Knocking on doors
And running away etc.

'Apologize!' shouts
The angry man
As Cranky shakes and sweats.
Cranky blurts out
The magic words,
Then out of that house he gets.

Knocking on doors
And running away etc.

Back at our desks
That afternoon,
Inside we both feel sick.
Even today
I hear those boots
Hitting the road with a click.

Knocking on doors
And running away
Try getting us if you dare
You won't catch us
'less you take a bus
And you can't afford the fare.

CLICK!
CLICK!

Astroten
Astronine
Astroeight
Astroseven
Astrosix

Astrofive

Astrofour

Astrothree

Astrotwo

Astroone

ASTRO NOUGHT!

!!!!!!!!   !!!!!!!!

!!!!!!!   !!!!!!!

!!!!!!!!   !!!!!!!!

The Fair

Splash of coloured lighting
Crash of loud guitars
Smash hits from the speakers
Bash of bumper cars.

Rash acceleration
Flash of yellow spark
Brash young racing drivers
Clash in summer park.

Cash out for the space ride
Slash the darkened sky
Gnash the teeth in terror
Mash the brain on high.

Lash out at the punchball
Dash around in carts
Splash the goldfish water
Gash the board with darts.

Stash the fair in trailers
Thrash the turf with vans
Trash the park, leave only
Ash and empty cans.

Tread on a Crack
and You Marry a Rat...

Tread on a leaf
and you marry a thief.
Tread on a slug
and you marry a thug.
Tread on a straw
and you marry a bore.
Tread on your lace
and you fall on your face.

Alphabet

A is for apple
So small and so square
B is for bucket
That flies through the air
C is for cup
You can eat it for lunch
D is for dragon
Which is put there to punch
E is for egg
So small and so square
F is for fish
That flies through the air
G is for grass
You can take it for walks
H is for hat
That whistles and talks
I is for igloo
So small and so square
J is for jam
That flies through the air
K is for kite
You can eat it for lunch
L is for lion
Which is put there to punch
M is for mummy
So small and so square
N is for nose
That flies through the air
O is for octopus
You can take it for walks

P is for plum
That whistles and talks
Q is for queen
So small and so square
R is for rat
That flies though the air
S is for sunshine
You can eat it for lunch
T is for target
Which is put there to punch
U is for umbrella
So small and so square
V is for vegetable
That flies through the air
W is for worm
You can take it for walks
X is for xylophone
That whistles and talks
Y is for yoghurt
So small and so square
Z is for zoo
That flies through the air.

You're It!

(for Mark)

I make castles
You be ghost.
I kick football
You be post.
I play teacher
You be taught.
I play crime squad
You be caught.

I play tag chase
You be it.
I play kick box
You be hit.
I play hero
You be man.
I play film star
You play fan.

I play farmer
You be pig.
I play doctor
You be sick.
I play leader
You be led.
I play soldier
You play dead.

Roads and Places

Secrets

I wrote a secret message
In lines of secret ink
So no one could discover
The secret words I think.

I took the secret message
When no one else was in
And secretly I hid it
Inside my secret tin.

I found a secret tree-trunk
Which held a secret fold
And slipped my secret package
Deep in the secret hole.

When I had grown much older
I sought the secret tree
To see if I could find the tin
Which held the secret me.

But all the trees looked taller
And changed a lot somehow.
They looked at me as if to say,
'Your secret's secret now.'

Lovers' Lane

Boyfriends walk
Down Lovers' Lane
Squeeze their girls
Down Lovers' Lane
Tall dark trees
Down Lovers' Lane.
I'll not walk
Down Lovers' Lane.

Girlfriends walk
Down Lovers' Lane
Guys on arms
Down Lovers' Lane
Close their eyes
Down Lovers' Lane.
I'll not walk
Down Lovers' Lane.

Couples walk
Down Lovers' Lane
Games they play
Down Lovers' Lane
Carve their names
Down Lovers' Lane.
I'll not walk
Down Lovers' Lane.

Railway Track

We used to put coins
On the railway line
Which someone once said
Was a terrible crime.
It wasn't that we might have
Stumbled and died
But that the Queen's head
Would go thin and wide.

Haunted House

The house, it must be haunted.
It has that haunted look.
Like something I remember
From movies or a book.

The windows all are broken,
They hang like mouths agape,
And in the darkened doorway
I thought I saw a shape.

The house, it must be haunted.
The tiles are broken too.
The roof looks like a skeleton
With bones all poking through.

I've never seen a light on
Or heard a doorbell ring.
I've never heard a dog bark
Or seen a living thing.

The house, it must be haunted.
We had to find out why.
We climbed in through a window-frame
And walked around inside.

The plaster lay on floorboards
In living-rooms and halls.
The staircase wood was rotten
And paper peeled from walls.

The house, it must be haunted,
Though not by ghost or ghoul,
But by a host of children
Who should have been at school.

I saw the bits of paper
And wrappers left from sweets,
The 'I was here' in lipstick
Next to 'I love Johnny Keats'.

The cigarettes and bottles,
The cycle spokes and tyres,
The ashes of some magazines
Where someone lit some fires.

Most folk keep away from here
For fear of spook or mouse.
Which means the safest place to hide
Is in the haunted house.

In Our Garden

I cycled up the garden path
To go to London Town,
But when I reached the rhubarb patch
I had to go back down.

I built myself a rocket ship
From toffee tins and wood,
But when it came to blasting off
The rocket simply stood.

I had an ocean-going boat
Set sail behind the shed,
But every time I turned the wheel
I spied the land ahead.

I searched for hidden treasure troves
For coins and precious stones,
But all that ever hit my spade
Were rocks and doggie bones.

I rode a horse called Silver
My pistol packed a punch,
But just as I rode into town
My Mum called me for lunch.

Jubilee Road

I don't like going
Down Jubilee Road
Because Jubilee Road is rough.
The gardens are covered
In thistles and thorns
And motor-car parts and stuff.

I'd get home much quicker
Down Jubilee Road
But the big kids stand there and stare.
I could be kidnapped
On Jubilee Road
And no one down there would care.

Heaven

What happens in heaven?
Will I sit on a cloud?
Is walking or talking
Or jumping allowed?

Will I be on my own
Or with some of my friends?
Does it go on for ever
Or eventually end?

What happens in heaven?
Will I play a harp's strings?
I can't play piano
I can't even sing.

Who chooses the music
That angels inspire?
Who does the auditions
For the heavenly choir?

What happens in heaven?
Are the streets paved with gold?
Is it crowded with people
Who're incredibly old?

Will I know who I am?
Will I know what I'm called?
If I pinch myself hard
Will I feel it at all?

What happens in heaven?
Do I go through a gate?
What if I get myself lost
Or turn up too late?

Is my name on a list?
Is the gatekeeper nice?
Can you sneak in for nothing
Or is there a price?

Cathedral

The old stone stands praying
The arch starts hurraying
The building is saying
How great is the Lord.

The glass is displaying
The sun finds its way in
The windows are saying
How great is the Lord.

The organ is playing
The candle flame's swaying
The whole church is saying
How great is the Lord.

Ladies and Gentlemen

The Queen of May

Sally I kissed in the classroom
In 1959.
Her hair was like a field of wheat,
Her skin as smooth as pine.

Sally became the Queen of May
And I became her knight.
I stood beside her golden throne,
We both were dressed in white.

We danced around a pole of wood,
Our ribbons crissed and crossed.
We skipped beneath this coloured web
Until the winter frost.

I wonder where she's dancing now,
Her hair as wild as mist,
The girl who was the Queen of May,
The girl that I once kissed?

Rag and Bone Man

Mister Cox
Wide and tall
Shoulders like
A castle wall

Curving nose
Shining head
Thermos flask
Roll of bread

Grubby hand
Silver ring
Greasy mac
Belt of string

Mister Cox
On his own
Rusted pram
Rag and bone

Rag and bone
Rag and bone
Who will give him
Rag and bone?

Rag and bone
Cloth and steel
Broken toys
Twisted wheel

Empty vase
Dusty mat
Splintered wood
Battered hat

Kitchen sink
Cardboard box
Rag and bone
Mister Cox.

Cowboy

One day our teacher asked us
what we wanted to be
when we grew up.
So we said:
electrician
school teacher
banker
doctor
lawyer,
except for David Smith
who said
cowboy.
We all laughed.
But secretly
I admired him
for telling the truth.

The Teacher's Gift
(Margarette Nicholson, 1909–85)

Every time I tell the time
Or work out ten times two,
I open up a precious gift
Bequeathed to me by you.

You gave me names and numbers.
You taught me how to spell.
You told me how to hold a pen
And how to write as well.

You showed me how to read aloud
From books of red and blue.
You filled my head with goats and trolls
And tinderboxes too.

You planted seeds inside me
But did not see them grow.
A bell rings at the end of school
We pack our bags and go.

These words I scrawl on paper,
This shape upon my tongue,
Is made from things you gave to me
Way back when I was young.

Snogging

Colin's brother snogged a girl
for an hour, non-stop.
Didn't lift his lips once.
Didn't break for refreshments.
They were on a park bench
locked together like
a magnet and a fridge.
It could have been
an hour and a half
or an hour and seventeen minutes.
No one asked who had the watch.
We were all amazed.
We were led to believe that
this was some kind of a record.
An hour! Non-stop! Snogging!
How did they breathe?
How did they see?
Who gave the signal to end?
I don't think Colin's brother
did very well
at maths or English.
But he got an A*
for snogging.

54

Teddy Boy

Sammy was a teddy boy
His fringe fell down in curls
He had a velvet collar
The sort you saw on girls.

A tie thin as a shoelace
Black trousers tight as skin
His socks were fluorescent
His fingers full of rings.

I saw him in the park one day
When mum and I were there
He swaggered like a pirate
And gave a moody stare.

Mum thought this kind of fashion
Showed England gone to rot
'Dress like that,' she warned me
'And I'll burn the blinking lot.'

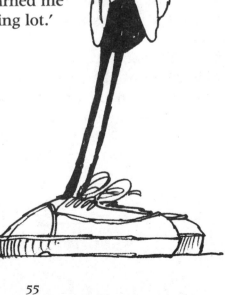

Stinker

A boy in my class we called Stinker,
For obvious reasons, I think.
We shuffled our seats to avoid him
And dodged from the drift of his stink.

He stood all alone in the playground
Hoping to be called to join in.
'Stinker! Watch out! It's Stinker!' we jeered
As if odour was something like sin.

I never knew why Stinker stank so,
Neglect, I assumed, like bad breath.
Years later I read in a paper
Of his early unfortunate death.

For the first time I learned he'd been ill –
His kidneys the cause of his shame.
I thought then of the things that I'd said
And felt the sharp sting of that name.

I saw the scene back in that classroom:
The blackboard, the chalk dust, the bell.
And there was me, part of the problem
For Dennis, known only by smell.

Miss Hart

Your skin
is so soft,
Your cheeks
are so pink.
No teacher
is prettier
Than you are
(I think).

You teach me
mathematics.
You help me
to spell.
I learn about
lipstick
And perfume
as well.

I'm only
a child
And you're
twenty-two
But I love you
Miss Hart.
I honestly do.

Bobby

When Bobby got angry
His face went bright red
The blood in his body
Went straight to his head.

He fought with his teachers
He pushed and he pulled
He clawed like a tiger
And charged like a bull.

They couldn't control him
But neither could he
He was trapped by his temper
And couldn't break free.

We gazed in amazement
And muttered, 'How bad.'
The fact is we liked it
When Bobby went mad.

News and Weather

Whether the Weather

When it rains
I stay indoors.
Spit. Drip. Drizzle. Pour.

When it snows
I go outside.
Spin. Drift. Flurry. Slide.

When it's cold
I wrap up tight.
Nip. Freeze. Chill. Bite.

When it blows
I hold my cap.
Howl. Roar. Whistle. Slap.

When it shines
I go half bare.
Burn. Scorch. Sizzle. Glare.

Christmas

We'll hang up our stockings
We always do that.
And I'll wake up early
I always do that.
There'll be a notebook and pen
I always get that.
And a chocolate bar
I always eat that.

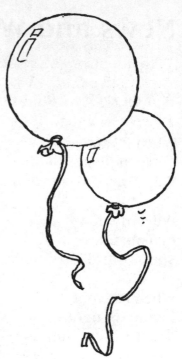

Then downstairs for breakfast
I always leave that.
We stand by the front room
We always do that.
Then Dad says, 'Come in'
He always says that.
And we sit with our presents
We always do that.

Then there's tearing and scrunching
I always hear that.
We say, 'Just what I wanted'
We always say that.
Then turkey for dinner
We always have that.
And mince pies for tea
We always eat that.

The thing about Christmas
I always think that
Is that it stays the same
Always like that.
And that's why I love it
I love it like that.
Everything else changes
But we always do that.

New Year's Resolution

It was January the 1st
I turned over a new leaf
It was clean on the top side
But had bugs underneath.

It's Fun to Have a Fever

It's fun to have a fever
To find myself in bed
When all the other children
Are off to school instead.

I peer between the curtains
And see them passing by
Trudging through the morning rain
While I am home and dry.

I prop myself on pillows
And wipe my sweating brow
It makes me feel much better
To think that maths is now.

Mum pours me some Lucozade
Then asks me what I need
I put on my dressing-gown
And go downstairs to read.

I sit beside the fireplace
And watch the flickering flames
My friends are having physics
Then French and double games.

It's fun to have a fever
As you can no doubt tell
So please don't send me greetings cards
That say things like GET WELL!

Fire!

Oh look, the fire-fighters
Rushing from their base.
We should see some sparks and flames
If we give a chase.

Oh look, the fire-fighters,
Racing up the hill
With their blue lights flashing.
This should be a thrill.

Oh look, the fire-fighters.
Now they're in our street.
Dad can see a thick black cloud
Rising fifty feet.

Oh look, the fire-fighters
Running though our door.
Yards of hosepipe in our house,
Water on the floor.

Oh look, the fire-fighters,
Fighting fire and smoke.
Forcing water onto flames,
Giving sparks a soak.

Oh look, the fire-fighters
Taking off their hats.
Mum is making cups of tea,
Dad just stands and chats.

Oh look, the fire-fighters
Leaving in their truck.
No more sparks and flames for us
With a little luck.

PC Buttle

I was throwing a snowball at an overhead light
When PC Buttle arrived.
I'd not heard the crunch of his oversized boots
As he sauntered up to my side.

'Could you explain to me what you're doing
   young man?'
Said PC Buttle to me.
'Er... trying to knock snow from that branch
   over there,'
I said, pointing up to a tree.

PC Buttle stroked his policeman-blue chin
And he knew that I knew I was wrong.
Would I be fined, imprisoned or taken back home?
No. He warned me, 'Just move along.'

In My Day

In my day
we got up at dawn,
made our own beds,
cooked our breakfasts,
walked to school,
worked hard,
didn't talk in class,
walked home,
enjoyed our homework,
ate all our food,
washed our plates
and went to bed early.
And told lies.

Get Off

Get off. Let me go.
Leave me alone.
If you don't get off
I'll shout. I mean it.
I'LL SHOUT.
Is it all right if I go now?
You're hurting me.
I should be home now.
I'm late. Let go. Let go… please.
GET OFF. OFF.
I'll be your friend.
I like you.
I didn't do it.
I mean, I didn't do
whatever it was
that somebody obviously did.
If you let me go
I'll get you some sweets.
What sweets do you like?
Please let me go.
I don't like being squashed.
Oh no! I think I'm fainting!
I feel sick.
If you let me go
I'll give you money.
I'll send you postcards
when I go on holiday.
Would you like to use my bike?
I've just seen a teacher.
I'm sure I did.
You're too heavy.

My ribs are cracking.
Don't sit on me.
I can't breathe.
I can't move.
I feel funny.
I feel dizzy.

My mum's a professional wrestler.

Thank you.

New Shoes

I loved my new shoes
And I treated them well,
From the curve of the heels
To the shine and the smell.

At night-time I kept them
By my bed on a chair,
So that if I woke up
I would know they were there.

I wore them like jewels
When I walked down the street,
With a face that implored
'Look at me and my feet!'

December 19th

The day after the day after tomorrow
I will then be able to say
That the day after the day after that
Is the day before Christmas Day.

Birth

I was born in a white house
At the end of September.
I cried on my arrival
The rest, I can't remember.

Body and Spirit

Who Am I?

I'm boy and child and brother and son
Him over there, the poetry one
Passport holder 41604
I'm all of these things, and much much more.

I'm legs and arms and body and head
A weight that makes a dip in the bed
A size that stands in front of your door
I'm all of these things, and much much more.

I'm skin and bone and muscle and brain
A pumping heart, a feeler of pain
A bundle of cells with ME at the core
I'm all of these things, and much much more.

I'm every thought that rises and falls
The face that stares from mirrors on walls
A secret code passed down from before
I'm all of these things, and much much more.

The Skull

Sometimes our playtimes
Were boring and dull
But not on the day
Some boys found a skull.

A real human skull
Found in the long grass
Where a ball had been kicked
Through too wild a pass.

They couldn't believe it
It looked like a stone
Except it had teeth
And was made out of bone.

On top of a stick
They stuck this old head
Then marched through the playground
Displaying the dead.

The yellow teeth grinned
From a bony white face
And eyesockets stared
Into bright morning space.

The skipping-ropes stopped
A hundred jaws fell
As everyone gazed
At this vision of hell.

This was adventure
Like pirates of old
This was much better
Than counting up goals.

Then Teacher came out.
It all had to stop.
Down came the stick
With the skeletal top.

A deep hole was dug
For the bodiless head
Then we all got told off
For disturbing the dead.

Hair and Teeth and Face and Hands

Get a little paste
Squeeze it on a brush
Rub it up and down
In a rush, rush, rush.
Don't forget your gums
And the difficult bit
Scrub it all around
And then spit, spit, spit.

Get a little sponge
Wet it in the sink
Rub it on your face
Till you blink, blink, blink.
Don't forget your ears
Don't forget your neck
Rub it round your cheeks
And then check, check, check.

Get a little soap
Hold it in a grip
Rub it in your hands
Until they slip, slip, slip.
Don't forget the dirt
Don't forget the ink
Wash away the suds
In the sink, sink, sink.

Get a little comb
Pull it through with care
Straighten out the strands
Of your hair, hair, hair.
Don't forget the back
Don't forget the top
Make it all look neat
And then stop, stop, stop.

Gingerbread Man

Gingerbread man
Stands with doughnuts and buns,
He waits in the window
For lunch-time to come.

Gingerbread man
Who could pull out your eye?
Who could watch as you crumble
With no way to cry?

Gingerbread man
Who could hold your sweet hand?
Then melt it with juice from a
Salivary gland?

Gingerbread man
Who could tear off your toe?
Who could stop you from standing
And injure you so?

Gingerbread man
Who could chew off your head?
Who could bite you and grind you
And leave you for dead?

Gingerbread man
I pass by you each day.
When I'm big I will save you
And hide you away.

Food

Cucumber, mustard,
Beetroot and swede,
Mashed-up banana,
Brown bread with seed,
Red peppers, olives,
Parsnips and cloves,
These are the foods that
I really loathe.

Elbows

Don't put your
elbows on the table.
You may need them
tomorrow at school.

With My Hands

Flap them in the air
    (wave)
Shove the ball away
    (save)
Smooth a doggie's fur
    (stroke)
Dig into a rib
    (poke).

Grasp another hand
    (shake)
Stick two bits of wood
    (make)
Squeeze an empty can
    (crunch)
Fingers in a fist
    (punch).

Slip a silver coin
    (pay)
Push them palm to palm
    (pray)
Test the water's heat
    (dip)
Hang on for your life
    (grip).

Push or pull a chair
    (shift)
Raise a weight up high
    (lift)
Press the button down
    (click)
Finger up your nose
    (pick).

Grab an arm or leg
    (catch)
Give an itch a bash
    (scratch)
Knock on someone's door
    (rap)
Thank you very much
    (clap).

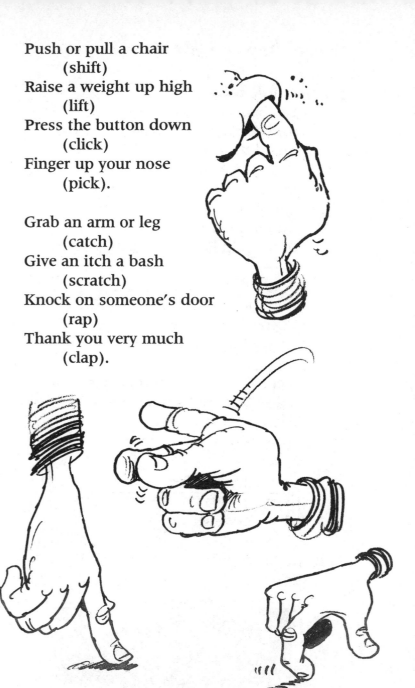

Ghost Story

A little baby ghost
Lay beneath a baby bed,
And do you know what
That little ghostie said?

It said, 'Mum. Come here.
Can you turn on the light?
I think I heard a noise
In the middle of the night.

'A mattress made a creak,
And then there was a snore,
Then I heard some feet
Go walking to the door.'

'Let's not have your nonsense,'
Said Mummy. 'Not a peep.
Humans don't exist
Now off you go to sleep.'

Ode to a Nose

O nose, who knows what I'd do without you
If my toes stank how could I tell?
How would I know when to wash my old socks
If not for your sharp sense of smell?

O nose, no time have you left me alone
You've stuck there like fruit on a bun.
You could have escaped a million times
For every nose knows how to run.

O nose, you know that I did not choose you
I did not vote 'yes' with a tick.
But, nose, you know if I started again
You'd be the first nose I would pick.

Backwards

I came into this world
at the age of eighty-one.
At seventy-eight I started school,
leaving for university
when I was just sixty-three.
I took my first job at sixty,
married at forty-five
and had two children.
I retired when I was twenty
so that I could spend
more time on my hobbies
and at ten I was put into
a young people's home.
At five I started forgetting things,
falling over and spilling my food.
At two I lost my voice.
By the time I was one
I could hardly walk
and had to be pushed around
in a chair with wheels.
In the end I was spending
most of my time in bed,
dribbling and sleeping,
crying in the night,
waiting to be born.

Animals and Insects

The Spider's Excuse

I'm a little spider.
Be not afraid, for I am good.
I wouldn't hurt a fly.
No. That's not true. I would.

Miss Muffet

Little Miss Muffet
Sat on her tuffet
Eating her curds and whey.
Along came a spider
And sat down beside her
and said, 'What's a tuffet?'

Hey Diddle Diddle

The cat was playing a fiddle they said
Or the fiddle was stroking the cat
But a cat has claws
On the ends of its paws
So how could a cat manage that?

The cow jumped over the moon they said
Or the moon slipped under the cow
But a cow has hooves
And it hardly moves
So I definitely don't see how.

The little dog laughed its head off they said
Or at least it chuckled and grinned
But happy dogs yap
Their tail bones flap
So the grin was probably wind.

The dish ran away with the spoon they said
Or the spoon fell in love with the plate
But a spoon would fall
If cuddled at all
So how could they go on a date?

The hey did a diddle, it did, they said
Or a diddle did something forbidden
But outside a riddle
A hey doesn't diddle
So I'd say the hey diddle didn't.

Hickory Digital Clock

Hickory digital dock
The mouse clicks on the clock
The clock comes on
A CD-ROM
Hickory digital dock.

Cat

I should like to be a cat
stretched out in the warm sun
puzzled by my shadow.
I would lick my chest
and scratch my ears
and no one would think it rude.
I would spend whole days
thinking about butterflies,
counting wing beats
and testing my claws.
I would curl up on cushions
and walk along walls.
I would tumble in bushes
and slide along roofs.
I would teach myself to purr
and hearing my purr
I would become happy
and purr even more.

Limerick

There was a young creature from space
Whose legs grew out of its face
The smell of its toes
Was so near its nose
It wore a clothes-peg just in case.

A Dog Called Nothing

I've got a dog called Nothing
That no one else can see
She doesn't play with strangers
She only comes to me.

I take her into classes
I walk her in the park
She never leaves a puddle
Or starts to bite or bark.

I keep her with me always
She curls up on my bed
The moment that I wake up
I stroke her faithful head.

So if you hear me calling
And all you see is air
You'll know that I'm not crazy
For Nothing's really there.

Thoughts and Dreams

*What Did You Want to Be
When You Grew Up?*

A pilot, a soldier,
A star of rock'n'roll,
A secret agent,
A digger up of coal.

A sailor, a surgeon,
The lead guitar or bass,
A detective, a film star,
An astronaut in space.

An explorer, a writer,
A deliverer of post,
An inventor, a painter,
A seeker out of ghosts.

A commando, a boxer,
A tearaway or tough,
An actor, stunt man,
A maker up of stuff.

That Little Word

What's that little word?
The one you just forgot?
The one you have to say
When you want something a lot?

What's that little word?
Do I have to give a clue?
Surely you remember
What it is you have to do?

What's that little word?
The one that starts with P?
The one that rhymes with bees
But doesn't rhyme with bee?

What's that little word?
I'm on my bended knees.
I'm begging you to say it,
So won't you say it, please?

The Wheel

Who invented the wheel?
What, why and where?
Were previous attempts
All pear-shaped or square?
Was it watching a stone
As it rolled down a slope
That gave the first wheelwright
His circle of hope?

Who invented the wheel?
We'd all love to know.
Did it take a long time
To make the thing go?
Did the neighbours all stand
And make stupid jokes
When they saw the first discs
With axles and spokes?

Who invented the wheel?
And what would they say
If they came back to life
And saw things today?
The jet planes and fast cars,
Moon buggies in space.
It's hard to imagine
The look on their face.

Why Are You Late for School?

I didn't get up
because I was too tired
and I was too tired
because I went to bed late
and I went to bed late
because I had homework
and I had homework
because the teacher made me
and the teacher made me
because I didn't understand
and I didn't understand
because I wasn't listening
and I wasn't listening
because I was staring out of the window
and I was staring out of the window
because I saw a cloud.
I am late, sir,
because I saw a cloud.

I Want to Be

I want to be just like all my friends
I want to be different too
I want to be a speck in the distance
I want to zoom into view.

I want to be a face in the audience
I want to be up there on stage
I want to be ignored and overlooked
I want to be all the rage.

I want to be followed by cameras
I want to be left on my own
I want to be where it's all happening
I want to hang out at home.

I want to be noticed by strangers
I want to vanish into thin air
I want to be the life of the party
I want to quietly stare.

I want to win handfuls of Oscars
I want to work with the poor
I want to make the grandest of entries
I want to slip out the back door.

The Future

The future? Yes, I remember it well –
Everything seemed so fantastic,
Everyone wearing helmets of glass
And sharp suits made out of plastic.

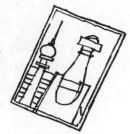

The skies were crowded with rockets and jets
With airborne buses and cars,
Meals were reduced to liquids and pills,
Vacations were taken on Mars.

We floated around with packs on our backs
And lived in a portable dome,
There was no need to use a duster or brush
With robots on hand in the home.

The future? Yes, I remember it well –
But it all seems so long ago
Back in the days of bubblegum cards
And black and white space-age shows.